P9-CFS-264

TOGETHER FOREVER!

True Stories of Amazing Animal Friendships!

Mary Quattlebaum

NATIONAL GEOGRAPHIC

WASHINGTON, D.C.

Since 1888, the National Geographic
Society has funded more than 12,000 research,
exploration, and preservation projects around
the world. The Society receives funds from
National Geographic Partners LLC, funded in
part by your purchase. A portion of the proceeds
from this book supports this vital work. To learn
more, visit www.natgeo.com/info.

For more information, visit
www.nationalgeographic.com, call
1-800-647-5463, or write to the
following address:

National Geographic Partners
1145 17th Street N.W.
Washington, D.C. 20036-4688 U.S.A.

Visit us online at nationalgeographic.com/books

For librarians and teachers:
ngchildrensbooks.org

More for kids from National Geographic:
kids.nationalgeographic.com

For information about special discounts for bulk
purchases, please contact National Geographic
Books Special Sales: ngspecsales@ngs.org

For rights or permissions inquiries, please contact
National Geographic Books Subsidiary Rights:
ngbookrights@ngs.org

Art directed by Callie Broaddus
Designed by Ruth Ann Thompson

National Geographic supports K–12
educators with ELA Common Core
Resources. Visit natgeoed.org/
commoncore for more information.

Trade paperback
ISBN: 978-1-4263-2464-2
Reinforced library edition
ISBN: 978-1-4263-2465-9

Printed in China
16/RRDS/1

Table of CONTENTS

Penny is a chicken. Roo is a dog. They became fast friends.

PENNY AND ROO: ON THE MOVE!

Penny and Roo met at the Duluth Animal Hospital in Georgia, U.S.A. They've been attached ever since.

Chapter 1

Hospital HELPERS

Dogs strain at their leashes. Cats meow in their carriers. A fluffy chicken scampers by in a diaper. Then a tiny dog wheels past in a special cart. The front desk of the Duluth Animal Hospital is busy! Many animals are brought here if they're sick or injured. The veterinarians (sounds like vet-er-ih-NAIR-ee-enz) here treat all kinds of animals.

Their patients include dogs, cats, hamsters, lizards, turtles, even chickens. They help their animal patients feel better or give them shots to keep them from getting sick.

But the chicken and the little dog—called a Chihuahua (sounds like chi-WAH-wah)—aren't patients. Penny and Roo work here. These two best friends welcome animal patients and their owners to the hospital in Duluth, Georgia, U.S.A.

The hospital staff appreciates their good work, especially Alicia Williams, their owner. Alicia works here as a receptionist. She helps patients prepare for their visit with the vets. So do Penny and Roo. Sometimes the patients are frightened or in pain. Their owners are worried.

But then Penny does something silly. She steals Roo's treat and trots fast, fast, fast on her feathered legs. Roo chases her and tries to grab the treat back. People smile and laugh. The two friends are so funny that they help everyone—animals and humans—feel more relaxed.

Penny and Roo have been working together for three and a half years. How did these two unique friends get this special job? Penny came first. Alicia met Penny when she was taking a class in animal science. Alicia had to learn about what happens when animals are used in research, and she had to visit some places that did this work.

Research is an important way to learn more about both animals and humans.

Here's how it works. Scientists study a small group of research animals. They give the animals in the group a special diet or medicine. Then they carefully observe, or watch for, changes in the animals. Do the animals grow bigger? Do they get better?

The scientists gather the information. They write papers about what they have learned and publish them. Other people can read about their research and learn how to improve the food they grow or the medicine they make or give. Scientists and doctors often learn about the effect of certain medicines on humans by looking at how the medicines affect animals.

Penny was a research animal in a study on diet. Alicia saw her on the last day of the study. Now that the research was done, the scientists would no longer need her.

Alicia looked at the young chicken. Penny was a beautiful hen! Instead of smooth feathers like most birds, hers were soft and fluffy. The feathers on her head and legs looked like a puffy hat and pants. Alicia wanted to give the hen a new home. "May I have her?" she asked the researchers.

And that's how Alicia ended up bringing Penny to the house she shares with her parents, three sisters, five dogs, two cats, and four parrots. Everyone in Alicia's family is an animal lover!

At first, Alicia didn't know how to care for Penny. Parrots and chickens are both birds, but they require different care.

There are more chickens—20 billion— than any other birds on Earth. They lay a trillion eggs a year.

Fancy Feathers

Silkies are unique chickens, with soft, silky feathers. They have black bones and black skin. They don't look very much like the jungle fowl that all chickens are descended from. One of their distant ancestors is the *Tyrannosaurus rex!* Silkies have some special traits. They have five toes instead of the usual four, and they have blue earlobes. They can't fly. Silkies like to brood, or sit on their eggs. They will even hatch the eggs of other birds.

Penny was also not a regular chicken. She was a fancy, gentle type called a silkie.

Alicia's boss, Dr. Mike Miller, was very helpful. He's a veterinarian. He told Alicia that chickens need special food and plenty of time outdoors. Alicia made Penny an outdoor pen so that she could scratch at the ground and search for bugs and seeds to eat.

But because Penny is very friendly, Alicia also made her an indoor pen. Chickens are flock animals and like to be with other chickens. With an indoor pen, Penny could be around the other pets and people in the house.

Penny quickly settled into her new home. Except that she didn't want to stay in her pen! She wanted to explore the house. But a chicken poops a lot, and Alicia didn't want to be cleaning up all the time. So, she tried putting a little diaper on Penny. It worked! Penny had her freedom, and Alicia didn't have a mess. What a good idea!

Now Penny could follow Alicia everywhere. She even learned to come when she was called. Alicia soon discovered that Penny loved to cuddle, too, unlike her parrots. Penny especially enjoyed sitting in Alicia's lap.

To show her pleasure, she would make a soft sound, like the purr of a kitten. But

Did You Know?

Chickens make many different sounds. A squawk might show fear, a purr contentment. A rooster's crow means "This is my territory." Hens often say *bawk* when they lay an egg.

when Alicia went to work, Penny was lonely. She missed her favorite human.

So, Alicia had another good idea: She would bring Penny to work. Penny and her boss thought it was a good idea, too.

Penny felt so comfortable at work that she soon started laying eggs at the hospital! Like Penny, these eggs are unique. Most chicken eggs are brown or white. Penny's are small and pink.

Everyone loved Penny! Penny received lots of cuddling and attention. She helped people learn more about silkie chickens. Many had never seen one before. "What's that?" kids would ask, pointing at the fluffy white hen. Sometimes they thought Penny was a kitten or a fancy dog!

When Penny first met Roo, he was in bad shape. She sat on top of him to warm him up. Soon, they both fell asleep peacefully.

Chapter 2

PUP in PERIL

One cold February night, Penny was at the hospital when a man rushed up with a small bundle. What was inside? A tiny puppy! The man had found the puppy in a ditch at a nearby park. He had scooped up the shivering creature and hurried to the hospital. The man had hoped the staff there could help. They always took good care of his pets.

The hospital staff was amazed. The puppy was so little! He was only six weeks old and weighed just two pounds (907 g). That's about the weight of a quart of milk.

He was missing the lower part of his front legs, several teeth, and a toenail. This pup would never be able to walk, run, or jump like other dogs. This dog could move from one place to another but only by dragging himself or hopping on his back legs. The puppy's way of moving helped inspire his name. He hopped like a kangaroo, so Alicia named him Roo.

Roo's past was something of a mystery.

Alicia thinks that Roo was tossed in the ditch by a dog breeder. The breeder had probably wanted to sell this puppy for a lot of money. When he realized that Roo had so many problems, he decided to get rid of the pup. Who would want such a dog? Alicia would! And Penny, too.

When Roo was brought to the hospital, the hen was resting in her soft, pink bed at the front desk. Alicia tucked Roo in beside her. The warmth of Penny's body would help warm and comfort the cold puppy.

Roo took one look at the big fluffy bird and pounced! The puppy began tumbling around. He chewed on Penny's feet and feathers. He wasn't hurting Penny, he just wanted to play!

"Penny wasn't sure what to think," said Alicia. "But when Roo settled down for a nap, Penny climbed on top of him, as if he were an egg. She warmed him up, and then they both slept."

They've been best friends ever since. They eat together and share water bowls. When it's time to go to the hospital, they travel in the same carrier. Sometimes they squabble like human brothers and sisters. They try to steal food from one another. Penny will steal one of Roo's dog treats, even though she can't eat it; and Roo will chase her.

Run, Penny!

Go, Roo!

What a game! The two play until they get tired, and then it's nap time. When they snuggle, Penny purrs, just as she does on Alicia's lap. Sometimes Penny even lays her eggs in Roo's dog bed. This is a way that Penny shows how much she trusts Roo.

Roo shares his toys with Penny, but his favorite plaything is still Penny's toes and fluffy feathers.

"Their friendship seems to be very unusual," said Alicia. Chickens are prey animals and dogs are predators. This means that chickens will try to avoid dogs. Dogs may chase or try to eat them.

Instead, these two friends look out for one another. Once Penny was sick for several weeks, and Roo stayed very close to her. He didn't want to play.

Small Dog, Big History

Chihuahuas are named for the state of Chihuahua in Mexico. A few of these dogs were found there, close to some ruins, in the 1850s. The little dogs may have an even earlier history, though. Carvings and artwork that are more than 1,000 years old show a larger Chihuahua-like dog called a Techichi (shown below). These dogs seemed important to the ancient Toltec and Aztec people of Central America. Some lived in temples and were buried in graves. Perhaps they were part of religious ceremonies.

And when Roo hurt his leg and needed surgery, Penny refused to leave him. She sat quietly by his bed until he recovered.

This is how Alicia explains the bond between Penny and Roo: "I think they were both little throw-away orphans in need of comfort and companionship, and they found that in one another."

Most of the other animals at Alicia's house ignore the two buddies—except for a pit bull named Lucy. She wants to take care of them. Lucy follows them around and bathes them with her tongue. Lick, lick, lick.

At 70 pounds (32 kg), Lucy is 14 times larger than Roo, but she always plays gently with him. She likes to poke and nuzzle. He likes to pounce and tug. Chihuahuas may be small, but they are definitely spunky!

Penny is part of the fun, too. She enjoys perching on Lucy's back. She gets a nice ride that way.

And Lucy never jumps or tries to knock Penny off. The big dog acts like a gentle mother to these two unique babies.

When they are working at the hospital, Penny and Roo stay in the reception area. "This is their domain," said Alicia. They greet animal patients, nap, and play with owners, their children, and sometimes the patients.

Yip, yip, yip, calls Roo in his squeaky voice. He's a noisy little rascal and likes to grunt, bark, and growl playfully.

Penny is quieter and makes a variety of chirps. When Penny seems restless and starts poking into corners and at the pet beds, Alicia knows what's going on.

Penny is getting ready to lay an egg! Alicia never knows exactly when or where this will happen, but she listens for a special sound. *Bawk!* calls Penny loudly. That means "I've laid an egg."

Penny and Roo are so much fun that people often schedule vet visits on the days when the two friends are working. People will sometimes make a special trip to see them. Some have even driven or flown from other states.

This special cart was donated to Roo so he could get around more easily.

When Roo was about six months old and had stopped growing, he was ready for wheels. A special cart would allow the little dog to move more easily. It would also help protect his back legs and hips. Roo would be able to sit up for the first time, too. Without such help, his front legs couldn't hold him up. He always had to lie down.

Humans often use wheelchairs if their legs are injured or don't work the way they should. This cart would be a kind of wheelchair for dogs. The only problem: These carts can be expensive. They are carefully made to fit each animal and to help their exact problems.

But Roo is one lucky dog! The owner of a patient at Duluth Animal Hospital heard about Roo's need. She wanted to give the little dog a gift: his own cart! She paid for everything.

Alicia measured Roo and sent the information to a company called Eddie's Wheels for Pets. They have helped big dogs and small dogs, from Great Danes to pugs. They even made a cart for a pet rabbit.

Surely, they could create the perfect cart

for Roo. In a few weeks, the cart arrived. It had two wheels and a little harness. It didn't weigh very much. Perfect for Roo, right? Roo wasn't so sure. He sniffed the cart. What was this strange thing? When Alicia fastened the harness on him, he froze. His eyes opened wide. *This feels weird*, he seemed to be thinking.

Did You Know?

In the 1840s, Queen Victoria of England received a gift of fancy Cochin chickens from China. She liked them so much that she collected more. They became so popular that many people wanted to buy and raise them.

Penny was as confused as Roo. She tilted her head first one way, then the other. She couldn't figure out this odd contraption.

Over the next few weeks, Roo practiced with his cart. Slowly, he learned

Did You Know?

It is not uncommon for a Chihuahua to suffer from phobias or fears, such as fear of being home alone, fear of traffic, and fear of unknown dogs.

how to move and turn it. He learned how to sit, too. Soon— *wheee!*—he was moving as fast as other dogs. He was on a roll!

The cart has made Roo very bold. Sometimes he tries to jump off the couch when he wants to get down. Sometimes he tries to climb the stairs. "He thinks there's nothing he can't do," said Alicia. "He seems to have no idea that he is different."

Roo is a little dog with a big spirit. He has places to go! Sometimes in his cart he moves so fast that he can't stop. *Whump!* He runs right into Penny, knocking her over. No problem! Penny just gives a little

cluck, jumps back up, and shakes out her
fluffy feathers.

Now that Roo has wheels, he and
Penny have a new job. They still go with
Alicia to the animal hospital, but they also
visit dog festivals and schools. Alicia, Roo,
and Penny help people learn how to take
care of pets.

They share information about being a
vet and other jobs with animals. Lively
Roo shows that disabled animals can lead
long and happy lives, with the help of
special carts and training.

And through their friendship, Penny
and Roo also teach something very
important. They show "how being
different can be a very special thing,"
said Alicia.

Pembroke Welsh corgi

Canine Cart

People have wheelchairs, why not dogs? That's what Ed Grinnell thought when his dog, Buddha, lost the use of her back legs. Buddha could no longer sit, stand, or move around. Ed figured out how to create a harness and an aluminum cart. He used the wheels from his daughter's toy wagon. It worked!

Ed began making carts in his basement for other disabled dogs. He called his company Eddie's Wheels for Pets. Soon he had so many orders, he had to hire and train others to build carts. Today, Eddie's Wheels for Pets makes about 2,000 special carts every year for dogs all over the world—and for cats, goats, and rabbits, too.

golden retriever

A goat and a donkey as friends? That's the true story of Mr. G and Jellybean.

MR. G AND JELLYBEAN: A STRANGE CASE!

What was troubling
the goat Mr. G?
At first, no one knew.

What was wrong with Mr. G? He refused to eat. He refused to move from the corner of his stall. When he first arrived at Animal Place, he was very curious. He sniffed the grass. He listened to the sounds of the nearby chickens. But within days of arriving, he wanted only to huddle in his straw and close his eyes.

The staff at Animal Place was worried. One day passed, then another. Was Mr. G sick? No. The veterinarian (sounds like vet-er-ih-NAIR-ee-en) had checked him. The goat needed to gain weight, but otherwise, he was fine.

Maybe he didn't like his new food. The staff talked to him gently. They tried to feed him treats and apples. Mr. G just turned his head. The skinny goat was getting skinnier.

Marji Beach had never seen a goat act like this, and she had seen a lot of goats.

Marji has worked at Animal Place in Grass Valley, California, U.S.A. for 12 years. She is the education director at this sanctuary (sounds like SANK-choo-air-ee) for goats, sheep, chickens, cows, and pigs.

Animal Place is a safe place for farm animals that no one wants. Sometimes the owner can no longer care for them. Sometimes the animals are old or have health problems.

Animal Place has fields where they can roam and play. It has sturdy sheds and barns where they can rest at night. Most animals that come to live here are happy.

Mr. G's behavior was a mystery! Marji and the other staff thought hard about how to help him. They knew Mr. G had lived almost all of his life—nine years—in the same place. It was a dirt lot in Los Angeles, California, U.S.A.

His owner hadn't cared for him properly. There had never been enough food or grass to graze. That's why Mr. G was so thin. Goats also like to play and explore. But the only plaything for Mr. G had been a rusty old car that he would climb and jump from. There was no shed to protect him from the rain or hot sun. At night, he always slept outdoors.

His new home was very different. At Animal Place, Mr. G had his own stall, clean straw bedding, plenty of food, and a big, grassy pen. But none of these things seemed to help Mr. G.

Four days passed, and Mr. G grew weaker and quieter. The staff wondered: Was he missing someone or something from his old home?

Marji called the officer who had rescued Mr. G. He had discovered a valuable clue. "What did you notice?"

she asked. The officer told Marji something important. Mr. G had lived in that dirt lot with a donkey named Jellybean.

When Mr. G was being driven away to Animal Place, Jellybean had become very upset. The female donkey—or jenny—had chased the truck, braying loudly. It had sounded like she was screaming!

"We realized then that Mr. G and Jellybean had a deeper bond than we had originally expected," said Marji. The staff began to plan. They wanted to bring the two friends together, but how?

Jellybean now lived at another sanctuary, 425 miles (684 km) away.

Someone would need to drive there and pick her up.

Animal Place had to plan for Jellybean's arrival, too. There had never been a donkey or a horse at the sanctuary, and Marji knew that they required different food and care.

Jeff McCracken, one of the volunteers at Animal Place, wanted to help. He volunteered to be the driver. It was a long ride to Jellybean's sanctuary. When he finally arrived, the staff took Jeff to Jellybean. What he saw surprised him.

He noticed that the donkey's head was down. Jellybean wasn't interested in any of the other animals or humans there. She seemed lonely. Could she be missing Mr. G, too?

Fine Dining

True or False?
Goats eat trash and cans.

False! Goats prefer leaves, twigs, weeds, and prickly briars, thank you very much. They enjoy dining on many plants that other animals can't digest. Like cattle and sheep, goats are ruminants, with four stomach compartments. They spit up and re-chew their food (called cud) several times until it is digested. More people in the world drink milk from goats than from cows. What a goat eats, though, can affect the flavor. Imagine a big glass of goat milk after the goat has eaten wild onions!

There was only one way to find out. Jeff knew he had to load Jellybean into the trailer and bring her to Animal Place.

But Jellybean refused to enter! She did not like that small space. She did not know this strange man.

People call donkeys "stubborn," but they are actually very smart. As a species, they survive in the wild by being alert to danger. They observe their surroundings carefully and try to figure out what might be wrong.

If a place seems unsafe, they will refuse to enter. It doesn't matter if a human wants them to go somewhere or do something— donkeys will decide on their own.

Donkeys will plant their hooves and refuse to budge. *No way,* they seem to be thinking. Other domestic animals, like horses, tend to be more obedient.

Jellybean was a true donkey! But Jeff knew that patience (sounds like PAY-shuns) was important in a case like this. He wanted Jellybean to trust him and to feel safe.

That's why Jeff did not try to pull or force Jellybean. He spoke to her calmly and offered her some sweet grain.

He hoped Jellybean would feel at ease. Jellybean eyed Jeff warily, but she ate some of the treat. Crunch, crunch.

Finally, Jeff was able to coax (sounds like COKES) Jellybean into the trailer. He breathed a sigh of relief. Now they could be on their way. They began the return trip to Animal Place. He hoped the plan would work.

Jellybean the donkey may not have realized just how much Mr. G the goat was missing her.

Back at Animal Place, Mr. G knew nothing about these plans. He lay quietly in his straw, with his head down. He didn't care that it was a sunny day or that the other farm animals were busy outside. When Jeff's truck drove up, the staff gathered to watch Mr. G. Oh, they hoped their plan would work! Mr. G heard the truck. He heard voices and the clomp-clomp of hooves. Then he slowly lifted his head and gave a big sniff. And then another. His eyes opened wide.

He could smell his friend, but did that mean she was close by? Mr. G jumped up to investigate. He raced to his stall door—and whom did he see, right outside his pen? Jellybean!

Mr. G ran to the fence. When Jellybean entered the gate, he raced to her side. He was so excited! "He leaped for joy and pranced around," said Marji. Jellybean was quieter, but "she kept a close eye on Mr. G."

The goat trotted around his buddy as if showing her around. They had been apart for six long days, and Mr. G didn't want to let her out of his sight. Within

Did You Know?

In 1785, the Spanish King Charles III sent George Washington a valuable Spanish donkey. Washington named it Royal Gift.

20 minutes, he was eating from a big bowl of food—and sharing it with Jellybean. The mystery was solved!

The next step for the two friends was to get to know their new home and the other farm animals. Mr. G and Jellybean began exploring the sanctuary's 600 acres (243 ha). Soon Jellybean was adding her loud hee-haw to all the moos, oinks, and clucks there. She may be the only donkey, but she's hard to miss. Her bray is big and sassy!

Now, the two friends spend their days together in the pasture, with nine other goats. They graze on tasty grass and relax under the shady trees.

Hee-Haw History

Donkeys have been helping humans for more than 6,000 years! On their sturdy backs, they carry people, bundles, and jugs of water. The first donkeys were desert animals. Certain traits helped them thrive in hot, sandy places and to survive harsh conditions in other parts of the world.

A donkey's narrow hooves help it walk on rocky trails and over rough ground. The light brown or gray color of a donkey's coat allows it to blend into the desert surroundings. It's harder for predators to spot. The color also reflects the sun and helps a donkey stay cool. Donkey teeth are especially strong. They are shaped to chew the tough grasses that many animals cannot eat.

Goats like to eat the leaves and twigs of shrubs and trees. This is called browsing. Here, Mr. G can also find and nibble on his favorite snack—oak leaves.

And there is so much to do! Mr. G can play with the other goats. He can poke at a fallen branch and climb rocks. No more boring dirt lot! No more rusty old car!

But Mr. G never strays too far from Jellybean. If the herd ever wanders too far from the donkey, Mr. G races back to her side. And if Jellybean moves too far away, get ready for some noisy bleating!

"Mr. G starts yelling, like he's injured," said Marji.

Jellybean will come rushing over,

thinking that her friend is hurt or in danger. When she realizes it's a trick, she gives Mr. G. a quick nip, as if scolding him. But Mr. G doesn't care. "When he wants Jellybean's attention, he'll do anything to get it!" said Marji.

At night, the two friends sleep in cozy, separate stalls because Jellybean sometimes gets restless. But these best buds can always see, smell, and hear one another. The staff knows this is important.

And now that the pair is settled in at Animal Place, Jellybean considers it her job to protect all the goats—especially Mr. G. In some parts of the world, donkeys are used to guard goats and sheep. They will rear up, kick, and chase dogs and coyotes that might threaten their herds.

Jellybean takes her work very seriously. She often patrols the pasture, checking for predators.

Jellybean keeps a sharp eye on the sanctuary's friendly pet dogs, too. And she even watches the way the goats treat one another. If she thinks that one goat is being too rough, she will give him a sharp nip. *Behave!* she seems to be saying.

Usually, though, the goats are friendly toward each other. They enjoy touching, nibbling, and licking one another. This friendly behavior is called "social grooming." That's how goats show that they like another creature—whether a goat, a person, or a completely different type of animal.

"Mr. G would love to groom Jellybean, but she is not interested," said Marji. Instead, the jenny shows her affection the way donkeys do. She guards her friend the goat and sometimes lets him touch her.

And Mr. G shows that he cares not by grooming but by standing close to her and following her. "The goat calls to Jellybean when he's sick," Marji explained. And he finds it hard to settle down and get better unless he can see the donkey.

But Jellybean does show her affection in one surprising way. "She will willingly share her grain with Mr. G," said Marji. "And she does not even like the Animal Place staff to get near her food bowl!"

Jellybean and Mr. G share food from the same bucket. Now that's friendship!

NEW FRIENDS

Most goats are bold and curious, but Mr. G is very shy. Because he never knew other goats or friendly humans in the dirt lot, at first he felt nervous with them at Animal Place. He wanted only to be around Jellybean.

Slowly, though, he began approaching the other goats. He began grazing closer to the herd. Then one day he noticed a new female goat—or doe—called Verna. She was recovering from surgery. She was very tired and quiet. Mr. G approached Verna gently. He lay down beside her, keeping her company.

Mr. G soon became Verna's first new friend at Animal Place. When she felt better, he introduced her to the rest of the herd. Sometimes goats will head-butt or push around a new goat, but Verna was accepted right away. *She's a friend of Mr. G's, so she's a friend of ours*, the goats seemed to think.

Did You Know?

Donkeys and goats make good companions for nervous horses. The big animal calms down when a small buddy is near.

And Verna helped Mr. G, too. He was learning to be part of a herd. He was realizing that, *hey, goats can be fun!* Soon, Mr. G became curious about another goat. This one was small and brown, with a long, flowing beard. He was gentle and affectionate. No wonder his name was Sweet Pea!

Mr. G started inching closer and closer to Sweet Pea. He nuzzled the goat. Sweet Pea nibbled back. Sweet Pea liked to snuggle and be groomed. So did Mr. G!

Soon the two goats were spending more and more time together. Now Mr. G had three good friends: Jellybean, Verna, and Sweet Pea.

The changes in Mr. G are "a real surprise," said Marji. They show how animals can overcome early fears and neglect if they are treated kindly.

Marji has seen positive changes in other animals as well. Since being founded in 1989 by Kim Sturla and Dr. Ned Buyukmihci, Animal Place has tried to give hurt or abandoned farm animals a better life. The staff watches each animal carefully to make sure it is thriving.

Many people think that sanctuaries are for wild animals that require protection from hunters. They know about sanctuaries for elephants, gorillas, tigers, and other wild animals. But what about cows, goats, sheep, and pigs? What about chickens and turkeys? People often don't realize that the animals that live on a farm might need protection, too. But the people at Animal Place believe that farm animals that need help should have a safe home.

Animal Place is that safe home. Some animals were found under terrible conditions. A cow named Panda once suffered terrible burns. A mischievous pig named Marigold was found as a frightened baby on a city street.

Now Panda and his cow pals ramble and graze in the green fields. Marigold and the other pigs dig at the ground with their snouts. Chickens peck at bugs. Turkeys strut. There are no tiny cages and nothing to be afraid of.

Did You Know?

Goats are strong climbers and jumpers. Some can climb trees and leap up to five feet (1.5 m).

The two best friends Mr. G and Jellybean will be at their new, safe home, together, for the rest of their lives. And so will about 300 other animals.

Do Animals Feel Emotions?

Do animals feel joy and sorrow? And do they feel these emotions in the same way as humans? Scientists are trying to find out. They have discovered that dogs "laugh" or make a kind of huffing sound when they play. Other scientists have looked at how animals react when a friend or relative dies. Do they grieve? Dr. Barbara J. King noticed that dogs, cats, elephants, and baboons seem to mourn. They might sit alone, refuse to eat, or make sounds of distress. Even ducks seem to feel a sense of loss.

Many people visit Animal Place every year. They like seeing the farm animals in good health, with lots of room to live and play. They learn how to treat farm animals and learn to appreciate their beauty.

Because of their unusual story, Mr. G and Jellybean have become known all over the world. They have been written about in articles. They have appeared on TV news shows. The goat and the donkey are stars!

Scientists are also becoming interested in friendships like Mr. G and Jellybean's. Why might two animals from different species (sounds like SPEE-sheez) form a bond that lasts over time? Who makes the first move? How do they communicate? How do they get used to another species?

There are lots of questions as scientists seek to better understand animal behavior and bonds.

Dr. Barbara Smuts noticed that it can often take time for a cross-species friendship to form, especially when the creatures are not in the same family of animals. She observed her dog, named Safi, trying to befriend the neighbor's donkey, Wister. At first Wister would chase Safi away because donkeys view canines as threats. Safi kept trying to visit, though, and over time, Wister came to trust her.

But with young animals, these bonds may form more quickly. They are often more open to making friends across species, according to Dr. Marc Bekoff, who studies animal emotions. When raised together, puppies, kittens, and sometimes even rabbits and birds play together. They will snuggle and groom one another rather than attack or flee, as they probably would in the wild.

This might explain why Mr. G and Jellybean are so close. Mr. G was very young when he first met Jellybean. "They were all alone in a boring dirt pen with no social interaction with other animals of their own kind or humans," said Marji. "They turned to each other for companionship."

Those hard times are now in the past. Mr. G and Jellybean have one another and their new friends. Jellybean shakes her head in a satisfied way. Mr. G nibbles an oak leaf. Not a *baa-d* life. It's pretty great!

SIRI AND IRIS: BEST MATES!

Cheetah cub Siri plays with her new puppy friend, Iris.

Siri romps through the grass at her new home at the Taronga Western Plains Zoo in Australia.

Chapter 1

Becoming BUDDIES

This was a big day for little Siri. The cheetah cub was about to meet someone special. Her keepers at the Taronga Western Plains Zoo in Australia had planned this moment carefully. Siri's mother had rejected her almost at birth, so the keepers had been caring for the cub at the zoo hospital. But she was all alone. Her keepers knew she needed an animal friend her age to keep her company. They just needed to choose the right buddy.

The new animal trotted over to Siri and sniffed. Wag-wag-wag went her tail. *Let's play!* she seemed to say.

Siri hissed and shrank back. What was this strange black creature? Siri was used to the quiet humans who held her and fed her milk. She didn't know how to deal with a lively puppy. When the pup sniffed again, Siri swatted her. *Stay away!*

Wait a minute! Why put a puppy and a cheetah together? Surely, that friendship was doomed. After all, cheetahs are large members of the cat family. And cats and dogs are enemies, right?

Not always. At other zoos, puppies had been introduced to orphaned cheetah cubs.

Dogs tend to be calm and friendly, and they help calm cheetahs, which can be nervous, timid animals. At the other zoos, the cubs and pups played and slept together, just like siblings. The orphans learned how to behave with other animals, not just with the people who cared for them. The cheetahs wrestled, pounced, and ran with their dog pals. The dogs helped the cubs grow up to be healthy and contented. Then the orphans could get to know the other grown cheetahs at the zoo.

This is important because there are only 10,000 cheetahs left in the world. Through breeding programs at zoos, cheetahs can give birth to cubs and raise them in a safe place. This can help save the species from extinction.

Jen Conaghan, the cheetah supervisor at Taronga Western Plains Zoo, knew about these cub-pup friendships at other zoos. Taronga Western Plains Zoo has a strong breeding program, with nine grown cheetahs. But Jen had never paired a cub with a puppy before. Siri would be the first at the zoo—and in the large country of Australia—to have a puppy pal.

It can take time to make a new friend. Over the next few days, Jen brought the pup for short visits with Siri. The pup was named Iris, which is Siri spelled backward. Maybe that name would bring luck to the friendship.

But Siri continued to hiss and swat. She squealed when Iris came too close. Yet after a time, Jen noticed an important change: Siri began looking for Iris. When the pup came near, she sniffed her. She was becoming less fearful and more curious.

The next step was learning how to play. Because she had no brothers or sisters, Siri had never tussled or tugged. Jen wiggled a soft, blue toy on the floor in front of Siri. Wiggle-wiggle. Siri watched. Like most cats, she naturally wanted to catch a wiggling bit of "prey." She crouched and pounced. She grabbed the toy with her teeth. Jen grabbed the other end. Then Iris joined in. Tug-tug-tug. The cub and pup now knew a fun game!

Siri and Iris made up other games. When Iris gave her a friendly poke, instead of hissing or squealing, Siri playfully pushed back. Iris rolled on her back, and Siri tumbled over her. They grunted and wrestled. Siri purred. *Hey, this is fun,* she seemed to think.

Soon Siri and Iris were ready for the next step in their friendship—and in growing up. It was time to play outdoors. The two friends needed room to run and explore, so the keepers placed them in a grassy yard. Siri sniffed at the air. What exciting new smells! She smelled the green earth and the trees. The grassy yard was near the wildlife clinic. Siri could see other animals coming and going. There was so much to explore!

Speedy Hunters

Cheetahs are the fastest land animals.
They can run up to 70 miles an hour
(113 km/h), but only for short sprints. Their
speed helps them catch prey like rabbits
and antelope. Because they have lanky
bodies rather than bulky muscles,
cheetahs try to trip or bump into their prey
rather than overpower it like a lion.
Cheetahs must eat their kill quickly, before
other predators arrive. They lack the
strength to fight lions or to climb a tree
with their prey, like a leopard would. A
mother teaches her cubs to hunt by
bringing them an injured animal so they
can practice stalking and chasing it.

Siri had been raised in the zoo hospital, but wild cubs grow up on the grassy plains of Africa. The zoo yard was like a cheetah's native habitat or home in Africa. The grass felt soft on Siri's paws. The sun warmed her fur.

Cheetahs are used to hot, bright sun. In Africa, they hunt in the morning and evening. That way they don't compete with lions, which hunt at night. The black "tear lines" on a cheetah's face are like the black face paint on football players. They cut down on the sun's glare, so the cheetah can see more clearly. In a way, cheetahs have sunglasses built into their fur.

Did You Know?

Cheetah comes from the Hindi word *chita*, which means "speckled body."

Their fur protects them in another way, too. The spots help cheetahs blend in with their surroundings. Their fur looks like the shadows and sunlight on a patch of grass. Soon after birth, cubs grow tufts of fur, called a mantle, along their backs. This mantle looks like thick, waving grass. It helps hide, or camouflage, the cubs from predators.

Siri sniffed the grass. She slunk through her new yard like a wild cub. Iris ran up, panting. Siri gave her a gentle swat. Like the littermates she would have had in the wild, it was good to have her sister-pup to play with.

Zookeepers soon discovered that Siri loves playing with balls.

Chapter 2

PLAY Ball

Siri and Iris love balls of all sizes, according to Jen. They especially love to chase a large soccer ball. When Jen picks up a small, yellow ball and throws it, both animals take off running. They race after the ball to see who will get there first.

"For now, Iris may be bigger, but Siri is usually quicker," said Jen. That's because cheetahs are built for speed. This helps them catch fast-moving prey on the African plains. Their long tails help them turn quickly. The tail acts like a boat's rudder, enabling the cheetah to change directions swiftly. When an antelope swerves, a wild cheetah can turn, too, and follow.

Siri races for the ball on her strong, swift paws. Her short, blunt claws grip the ground, like soccer cleats. Most cats, including big cats like lions and tigers, have claws that retract, or pull in. They are good for fighting or climbing, but they don't help with running speed like a cheetah's do.

Iris scrambles for the ball, but Siri grabs it

Did You Know?

Cheetahs purr, growl, and chirp, but they do not roar like lions and tigers. They lack the necessary neck bone.

80

and zooms away.

"They are best mates," said Jen, using the Australian word for "friends." "They are rumbling and tumbling together every day." Sometimes Siri still squeals dramatically, but it is no longer a sign of fear. The squeal usually means that the cub is losing a wrestling match.

Siri and Iris love to play. In fact, many baby animals do, but why? Are they learning important skills? Yes. Iris has helped Siri "develop her natural social skills," said Jen. Iris helps Siri learn how to get along with other animals. Their play also helps both animals with "muscle development, strength, and speed," she said. "Normally, this would be practiced with littermates.

Helping Cheetahs Survive

A century ago, there were 100,000 cheetahs in the wild. Why do fewer than 10,000 cheetahs exist today? In the wild, cheetahs are at risk. Lions and hyenas prey on cubs while the mother is hunting. To protect them, a mother often moves her cubs to a new hiding place every few days.

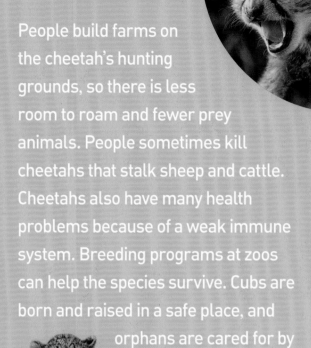

People build farms on the cheetah's hunting grounds, so there is less room to roam and fewer prey animals. People sometimes kill cheetahs that stalk sheep and cattle. Cheetahs also have many health problems because of a weak immune system. Breeding programs at zoos can help the species survive. Cubs are born and raised in a safe place, and orphans are cared for by humans. Every cheetah is special!

Iris has been a substitute (sounds like SUHB-stih-toot) sister for Siri."

Little predators like Siri may also be learning how to hunt and how to protect themselves. "The first 6 to 12 months is important for cheetah cub development," said Jen. "They must gain experience with stalking and hunting behaviors. Iris provides this opportunity."

Romp, tug, tussle. After a few weeks in the small grassy play yard, Siri and Iris had grown so much that it was time for the next move: to a bigger grassy enclosure (sounds like in-KLOH-zhur).

Siri looked around her new space. What were those lean, graceful animals in the nearby pens? More cheetahs! Iris and Siri's new home was the cheetah complex. This way Siri could get to know the zoo's other cheetahs. When grown, hopefully she would join them in the breeding program.

The adult cheetahs peered at the odd pair. They were interested in the cub, but they were really curious about Iris. *What is this little creature?* they seemed to be thinking. *Look at that wagging tail!* They had never seen such an animal.

In addition to cheetah neighbors, the friends' new pen had a large box. It was the perfect place to curl up together and sleep at night. The large pen had hills to climb, trees to sniff, and logs to explore.

Did You Know?

Cheetahs have excellent eyesight. In the wild, they often climb on top of a log or termite mound and scan for prey.

And it had something else that both animals love: a small swimming pool!

Pet cats may not like water, but cheetahs do. Africa is very hot, so wild cheetahs enjoy a cooling dip in a pond. So does Siri.

On hot days in Australia, the keepers will turn on the sprinkler. Swish! Swish! Siri and Iris run through the drops and splash in their pool. They jump in puddles and wrestle in the wet grass. So refreshing!

At mealtime, each friend goes into her own space. The two are fed in the morning and the evening, and they have different diets. Iris gets dog kibble and bones, and Siri eats chicken, beef, and kangaroo meat.

Because they are different species, each animal needs the food that will best nourish her body and keep her teeth and jaws healthy. The pals lick their own bowls clean. And after every meal, Iris makes sure to give one last lick to Siri's bowl, too.

Jen watches the two buddies at different times of the day. She watches how they share toys and how they lick and groom one another. These are signs of bonding.

But Jen knows a lot about cheetahs and dogs. She knows that, besides diet, the two species have other different needs.

As they get older, Jen knows they will probably need to make changes in the pals' life together. She watches for even small changes in behavior. That way she'll know when the time has come.

Even as they grow,
Siri and Iris still love
playing together.

Chapter 3

A Cheetah's Best Friend

A big difference between cheetahs and dogs is that grown cheetahs are solitary (sounds like SAH-lih-tare-ee) animals. That means they prefer to live alone. Lions live in groups or prides, and the females hunt together. But a female cheetah lives and hunts alone, except when she has cubs. When she has cubs, they stay with her until they are

18 to 24 months old. Then they leave. As Siri gets older, she needs some quiet time away from Iris.

And dogs like company. They are pack animals, which means they prefer to live in a group. So Iris needs more, not less, company as she gets older.

Jen knows just what to do. To start, the friends' enclosure is not on view to the public. This ensures (sounds like en-SHORES) privacy for a young, nervous cheetah like Siri. And while Siri enjoys her quiet time, Jen takes Iris for walks around the zoo. Iris welcomes all the attention she receives on her walks. People stop to pat her. Kids crowd close to say hello. Wag-wag-wag goes Iris's tail.

Iris has met many other zoo animals. She likes to trot by the black rhinoceros. The Asian elephants extend their trunks, and the Galápagos tortoises rest in the sun as she passes by.

Like the cheetahs, all these animals are considered endangered or vulnerable, and they are all part of Taronga Western Plains Zoo's special breeding programs. Iris has also gotten to know the Addax antelope, with their long, curved horns, and the shaggy Przewalski's (sounds like sheh-VAL-skeez) horses.

"The pup never tries to frighten or chase the zoo animals," said Jen. She has learned basic commands like come, sit, and heel, so she is well behaved on her outings.

"Iris is one of the best-natured dogs

I have ever seen," said Jen. Like any young dog, she can be mischievous, but she also knows when to be gentle and calm.

This is important because Jen needs Iris's help with another tiny cheetah. It's a new cub named Jelani.

Like Siri, Jelani was the only cub born to her mother. Cheetahs usually give birth to three to five cubs. When only one cub is born in the wild, the mother usually abandons her baby. That's because a single cub often does not stimulate the mother to make enough milk. Like all mammals, cheetah cubs rely on their mother's milk for food.

When Jelani was rejected by her mother, the keepers took her in, just as they did for Siri. Jelani receives a bottle of special milk formula five or six times a day, and she goes home with a keeper at night. Soon she'll live full time at the zoo, like Siri.

The zoo staff likes to give names that reflect the cheetahs' native country, Africa. In Swahili, Siri means "secret." At first, Siri had been quiet, like her name. Jelani means "mighty" in Swahili, and this cub seems to be living up to her name, too. "Jelani is very bold," said Jen. "She shows no fear."

Knowing how much Iris helped Siri settle into her new home, the keepers wanted to introduce the pup to Jelani. At the time, Jelani was seven weeks old and weighed almost seven pounds (3 kg). But Iris was seven months old.

Top Dog

Who's Number One?

The Labrador retriever, according to the American Kennel Club. In the United States, Labs have been the favorite dog for more than 20 years. The breed is calm, friendly, intelligent, and easy to train. Labs make excellent service dogs, helping blind, deaf, and disabled people. They are popular pets. Labs are also hunting dogs. They were bred to retrieve ducks shot by hunters. Labs are strong swimmers, thanks to their large webbed paws and otter-like tails. Their two coats of short, dense fur keep them warm and dry even after a plunge into cold water.

Labrador retrievers can be blond, black, or chocolate brown in color.

She weighed almost 60 pounds (27 kg). She was a giant beside the tiny cub.

But Iris is a mix of two breeds that are very gentle. She is part mastiff, so she is large and easygoing, and she is part Labrador retriever, so she is calm and friendly.

Even at her size, Jen thought Iris would be the perfect first friend for a mischievous cub. At their first meeting, Iris lay down on the floor. She rolled over and remained quiet while Jelani sniffed and climbed on her. The cub scampered up and tumbled down. Iris was one amazing mountain of a dog! It didn't take long for the two to become friends.

Jelani and Iris now play together regularly. Iris nudges softly, but the cub tries to wrestle her big friend. There are no dramatic squeals. Instead, Jelani has discovered her favorite plaything: Iris's tail. Wag-wag-wag. Pounce!

Iris enjoys her new cheetah buddy, her keepers, and the zoo animals and human visitors she has met. But one of her favorite times of the day is still snuggling with Siri at night. The friends settle into their sleeping box, groom one another, and close their eyes.

In the future, Siri may need to separate from Iris. Her instinct may tell her to become solitary. Without her best mate, though, she could never have grown into a powerful cheetah with animal skills and instincts. She could not have developed into a healthy grown-up female able to give birth and raise cubs. And Siri helped Iris become a dog with an important mission: cheetah conservation.

There is an old saying: A man's best friend is his dog. But for Siri, a cheetah's best friend is her dog. And Jelani agrees!

THE END

DON'T MISS!

NATIONAL GEOGRAPHIC KiDS CHAPTERS

RASCALLY RABBITS!

And More True Stories of Animals Behaving Badly!

Aline Alexander Newman

Turn the page
for a sneak preview . . .

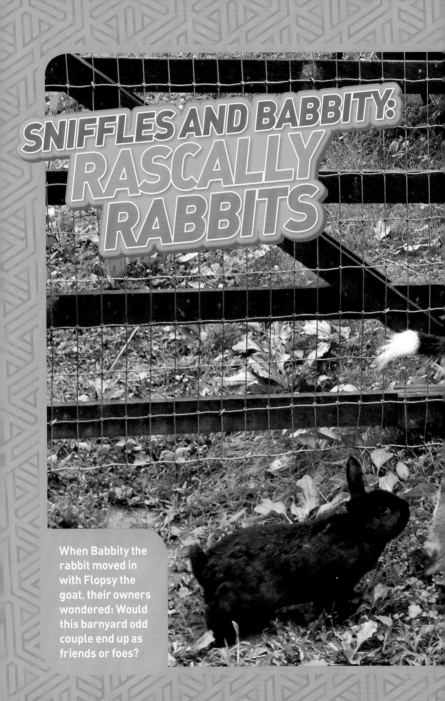

SNIFFLES AND BABBITY: RASCALLY RABBITS

When Babbity the rabbit moved in with Flopsy the goat, their owners wondered: Would this barnyard odd couple end up as friends or foes?

Sweet little Sniffles has soft fur, stiff ears, big eyes, and a supersize sneaky streak.

Chapter 1

Wade Newman had no time to waste. Night was falling in Turin, New York, U.S.A. And his rabbit, Sniffles, was missing. The 14-year-old boy had to find the little bunny before the evening turned too dark to see.

Wade searched his yard. He peered under bushes and poked into weeds. He looked behind the garage and on top of the woodpile. But snuggly Sniffles was nowhere to be found.

Earlier that afternoon, Wade had let the rabbit out of its hutch. His dog, Boo Boo, was running loose in the yard. So was Sparky the cat. *Sniffles needs to have his own adventure*, Wade thought.

It seemed safe enough. Wade lived in dairy-farming country. His family's house sat far back from the road. A creek ran along one side and a large cornfield bordered the other. Out back stretched a rocky cow pasture.

The only trouble was Sniffles' small size. He was a Netherland (sounds like NETH-er-land) dwarf rabbit and weighed just two pounds (0.9 kg). The little hopper could disappear in tall grass or hide inside a flower pot. *So where is he now?* Wade wondered. *I've always been able to find him before.*

Never once had he let Sniffles or Boo Boo stay outside all night. Sparky did sometimes stay out. Like all cats, Sparky had excellent night vision and enjoyed prowling in the dark. *If only I could see that well,* wished Wade. But he couldn't. When total darkness fell, he gave up looking for Sniffles.

Scary thoughts rushed through Wade's mind when he tried to sleep. *Was Sniffles lost? Had he been nabbed by an owl or coyote?* If only the rabbit had stayed in sight.

Did You Know?

The best way to pet a rabbit is to gently scratch its forehead and between its eyes.

Big Bunnies, Little Bunnies

From forests to deserts, rabbits live all over the world. People began taming them about 500 years ago. Today there are 48 breeds, or kinds, of tame rabbits. The breeds differ in color, looks, and type of fur.

But breed doesn't affect how friendly a bunny will be. So when choosing a pet, think about size. There are tiny, 3-pound (1.4 kg) "pocket pets" like the lionhead (shown here). And there are 20-pound (9.0 kg) checkered giants. Pick the bunny that you have room for, can afford to feed, and find easy to handle.

Morning finally came, and Wade's father found Sparky sitting on the back porch stoop. And, surprise! Beside him sat Sniffles! *How did that happen?* Wade wondered. *Were Sparky and Sniffles together all night? Or did they meet up at dawn?*

Wade would never know. But relief flooded over him as he scooped up his bunny and rubbed him against his cheek.

Sniffles had returned unharmed, so Wade continued to let him out of his hutch. "Don't go far, and come back before dark," he told the bunny. But did Sniffles listen? No! The naughty bunny missed curfew many times. Wade learned not to worry and just wait until morning. Then Sniffles and Sparky would appear at the door.

But Sparky was old, and he eventually

died. Everyone missed him, including Sniffles. The bunny had lost his friend and his guide. Wade worried that without Sparky, Sniffles might not find his way home. So Wade stopped letting the rabbit loose in the yard. He began bringing him inside the house instead.

Wade usually did this at night, when he lay on the couch and watched TV. Then Sniffles would crawl inside one of Wade's pants' pockets and sleep.

One night, Wade was focused on his TV show. He failed to notice when the little rabbit started chewing. Chewing is a natural behavior for rabbits. So doing it must have felt good to Sniffles. But he nibbled a big hole in Wade's best pants. Oops!

Other problems came up. Hopping around outside used to wear down Sniffles' nails. Now that he no longer did that, his nails grew too long. Wade's mom tried to cut them. But Sniffles wriggled and squirmed. Once she cut too deep by mistake, and it made the rabbit's toe bleed.

Sniffles was acting different, too. He used to show joy by jumping straight up and to the side. But the bunny stopped doing his happy dance.

Wade hated to see Sniffles so sad. So he took a risk. He started letting Sniffles run loose outdoors again.

All went well for a while.

Want to know what happens next? Be sure to check out *Rascally Rabbits!* Available wherever books and ebooks are sold.

INDEX

MORE INFORMATION

To find out more information about the animals featured in this book, check out these articles and websites:

Penny and Roo

Why Did the Chicken Cross the World? by Andrew Lawler (NY: Atria Books), 2014.

American Kennel Club www.akc.org.

American Silkie Bantam Club www.americansilkiebantam club.org/about.

Eddie's Wheels for Pets www.eddieswheels.com.

Mr. G and Jellybean

Animal Place www.animalplace.org.

Donkey Breed Society www.donkeybreedsociety .co.uk.

National Zoological Park, Smithsonian Institution, "Goats fact sheet," nationalzoo.si.edu/Animals/ KidsFarm/InTheBarn/Goats/ factsheet.cfm.

Siri and Iris

"So You Think You Know Why Animals Play," by Lynda Sharpe, *Scientific American* guest blog, May 17, 2011.

Taronga Western Plains Zoo www.taronga.org.au/ taronga-western-plains-zoo.

To Judy Leaver, an amazing friend.
—MQ

CREDITS

Cover: Toby Zerna/Newspix/REX Shutterstock; 4-5, Alicia Williams; 6, Alicia Williams; 12 (UP LE), Stephan Westcott/Getty Images; 16, Alicia Williams; 22 (LO LE), Danita Delimont/Getty Images; 26, Alicia Williams; 32, Custom Life Science Images/Alamy Stock Photo; 33,Elizabethsalleebauer/RooM the Agency/Corbis; 34-35, Marji Beach/Animal Place; 36, Marji Beach/Animal Place; 43, Dustin Jensen/Getty Images; 46, Marji Beach/Animal Place; 50 (UP LE), Horizon International Images Limited/Alamy Stock Photo; 51 (LO RT), Wild Wonders of Europe/Geidemark/NPL/Minden Pictures; 56, Marji Beach/Animal Place; 62 (UP LE), David Baileys/Getty Images; 66-68, Toby Zerna/Newspix/REX Shutterstock; 75 (UP), Mint Images - FransLanting/Getty Images; 78, Toby Zerna/Newspix/REX Shutterstock; 82 (UP) and 83 (UP), Suzi Eszterhas/Getty Images; 83 (LO), Roger de la Harpe/Getty Images; 88, Toby Zerna/Newspix/REX Shutterstock; 94, Purple Collar Pet Photography/Getty Images; 94, Jim Craigmyle/Corbis

ACKNOWLEDGMENTS

Many thanks to the following people who helped with this project:

Shelby Alinsky and Brenna Maloney, my two amazing editors.

Jen Conaghan and Kellsey Melhuish of the Taronga Western Plains Zoo in Dubbo, New South Wales, Australia, for contributing so many wonderful details about Siri, Iris, and Jelani. www.taronga.org.au/taronga-western-plains-zoo

Marji Beach at Animal Place for her expertise and kind aid with the Mr. G and Jellybean story. www.animalplace.org

Alicia Williams for her generous assistance with the tale of Penny and Roo and to the Duluth Animal Hospital for the special care given to all its animal patients. www.duluthanimalhospital.com

Ed, Leslie, and Chris Grinnell for kindly sharing information on disabled animals and Eddie's Wheels for Pets. www.eddieswheels.com

My supportive, good-humored family.